THE AUTHOR INCOME PROBLEM

TRACK YOUR SALES WITHOUT PULLING YOUR HAIR OUT

M.L. RONN

Published by Author Level Up LLC.

Version 3.0

Cover Design by Pixelstudio.

Covert Art © ingka.d.jiw / Depositphotos

Editing by BZ Hercules.

Warm thank you to a special group of people who helped me on my sales journey to solve this problem: Tom Donahue, Olga Kirshenbaum, Dale L. Roberts, and Oz du Soleil. This project wouldn't have happened without their coaching and guidance.

Special thank you to the following people on Patreon who supported this book: Jon Howard, Megan Mong, and Lynda Washington.

Some links in this book contain affiliate links. If you purchase books and services through these links, I receive a small commission at no cost to you. You are under no obligation to use these links, but thank you if you do!

For more helpful writing tips and advice, subscribe to the Author Level Up YouTube channel: www.youtube.com/authorlevelup.

WHY I WROTE THIS BOOK

Authors have a lot of problems: we have to learn how to write better, write faster, and market our books, among many things.

But there's another problem that stands above all the rest.

When you start selling books, how do you track your author income?

I've written over 50 books, and I make money every month from many different book retailers. I sell books in ebook, paperback, audio, and three languages. I make money on YouTube through advertising revenue and brand deals. I have an audience that supports me on Patreon. I promote at least 20-30 different products and services, all of whom pay me affiliate commissions every month. I also sell online courses and make direct sales with my readers. And I haven't even gotten into consulting fees and other miscellaneous income!

Somewhere around book six, I realized that I needed to get organized because going through my income statements every month was time-consuming and difficult. My time is too important to spend hours in Microsoft Excel doing tedious data entry. I should be *writing*.

I tried everything to solve this problem, and I mean *everything.*

I found a cute little Excel spreadsheet that another author shared with the community. It was a great spreadsheet except for the fact that each tab represented one book. Imagine a spreadsheet like this for 50 books!

I hired an Excel guru to build me a better spreadsheet. He created an improved spreadsheet with a nice dashboard that did help me for a little while, but I still had to manually enter my sales data into the spreadsheet, which made me stop using it.

I even hired an assistant to calculate all of my sales each month. After the third month, he quit because he hated the job. I've talked to virtual assistants about this problem: it turns out that none of them enjoy "doing" a client's book sales—hence, why my assistant quit. This is one job that you truly cannot outsource without causing sheer mental and physical pain to another person.

I tried different sales tools that I found on the Internet—none which shall be named—and while they were each decent in their own right, they had significant shortcomings. One of them required all of your retailer website logins, which is a nonstarter for me. Another was Amazon-only. Yet another was Windows-only. I'm a Mac user.

With so many options that didn't suit my situation, I simply gave up and stopped tracking my sales for several years. Sure, I had an *idea* of what I was making per month, but I didn't have the full picture—certainly not what I was making per month *per book.*

When you have as many books as I do, this is the number one problem you must tackle in your writing business.

And yes, I'm 100 percent serious. This problem is worse than building an audience or learning how to sell books. If you learn to do those things, you'll create a flood of money. Most people would say that a "flood of money" is a nice problem to have, but if you fail to *manage* your money, you will drown in that flood.

If you don't understand where your money is coming from, you can't truly call yourself a business owner. Think about a restaurant, or a flower shop, or a convenience store. Do they ignore their income? Absolutely not. They know their income to the penny, and which products are driving it.

Authors and creative entrepreneurs are the only profession I know of that have such a lax mindset about money. We tell ourselves "it'll just work out," when in reality, it won't if we don't face the problem.

If you don't know where your money is coming from, you cannot manage your money—your money manages you.

You also can't make accurate marketing decisions. What if one of your books was selling a decent amount out of nowhere, but you didn't find out until several years later, when it was too late to capitalize on the moment? That happened to me several times.

Or, what if you changed the book cover for one of your books, and instead of improving your sales, it actually harmed them? That happened to me too.

Maybe one of your series was performing well, but sales have been slipping over time. If you recognize the warning signs, you can do something about it before it's too late. I, too, have made this mistake.

It's embarrassing for me to admit these mistakes, and quite frankly, I risk my reputation as an influencer in even writing about them since I talk all the time about treating your writing as a business. But the hard truth is that many in the writing community struggle with this problem—*particularly* successful authors.

In researching this book, I can't tell you how many

successful writers I talked to who told me that they don't track their sales, or they pay an assistant to do it for them (which means they still don't track their sales), or they settle for an incomplete or unsustainable solution.

All of these authors admitted that sales tracking was a problem, but they didn't know how to solve it.

In January 2020, I decided that I had had enough. For the first time in my author business, I was finally making a significant amount of money. Several of my books had taken off and my YouTube channel, Author Level Up, was bringing in sizable income each month.

Yet I had no idea what was going on. I felt out of control.

I was tired of not knowing my sales data, and more tired of Excel data entry.

I swore that I would solve this problem for myself once and for all, and that I would dedicate brainpower and money to solving it, even if it meant publishing fewer books in 2020. I also swore that I would never do Excel data entry or inflict that pain on an assistant ever again. They were bold promises, but this problem caused me so much pain that I was willing to aim high.

As is the case with many of the problems I choose to solve, I found that I was *the only one* in the community talking about it. I underestimated how many writers were addicted to the KDP Select ecosystem. I also underestimated the extent to which writers don't feel they need to track their income because they've convinced themselves that they'll never be successful.

For those who *did* have a healthy relationship with money, however, most had just given up. Others were holding out for a convenient solution that was sure to come someday. A few brave authors were still fighting the good fight, spending 2-4 hours in Excel every month.

Little did I know that the journey I was embarking on

would take me well outside of the publishing community. I talked to hugely successful writers, book retailers, accountants, data analysts, world-renowned Microsoft Excel experts, and even money coaches.

And at the end of my journey, I solved the problem for myself. In fact, I solved it so thoroughly that I will never have this problem again.

But it wasn't enough for me to just solve it and walk away. I wanted to help other writers. So I wrote this book.

This book is a recap of everything I learned, and my vision of what the answer to the author income problem must look like if we are to tackle it as a community.

Some of the ideas in this book are odd, and opposite of what you would expect someone to say about this topic. Some of the ideas are so foreign that you may immediately reject them. That's okay. With time, hopefully I'll prove that my ideas are right—or at least, a step in the right direction.

But if there's one thing I've learned on this journey, it's that complicated problems require unconventional solutions. Sometimes those solutions are simpler than you think.

If you're ready for some major data geekery and a fun, circuitous route around "the author income problem," welcome aboard. In case you're unfamiliar with some of the terms in this book, refer to the Appendix, where I define many of the terms for your convenience. I'll do my best to explain them in the book itself too, but the Appendix will give additional context.

This book won't be the sexiest writing book you'll read, but it will be fun, and it will help you think about this problem in a different way.

THE GREAT RIDDLE

In ancient Greek mythology, the great city of Thebes was taken hostage by a Sphinx. With the body of a lion, head of a woman, and a gigantic wingspan, she menaced the entrance to the city, asking visitors riddles. If you solved the riddle, she let you in.

There were two problems: first, if you didn't answer the riddle correctly, the Sphinx killed you. Second, no one had ever solved the riddle, so you were almost sure to die.

Then came Oedipus, the famed Greek hero who taught us the unfortunate concept of self-fulfilling prophecies (he murdered his father and married his mother—you know, *that* guy).

In one of Oedipus's defining moments, he faced the Sphinx and answered the most famous riddle of all time: "What goes on four legs in the morning, two legs in the afternoon, and three in the evening?"

Of course, Oedipus's answer was "man."

When Oedipus solved the riddle, the Sphinx died, and he saved the city of Thebes. The residents immediately crowned him king.

You're probably wondering what this has to do with author income.

I argue that the author income problem is the author community's version of the Sphinx. Only a few have solved her riddle. Too many authors have gotten their heads bitten off, so nobody goes to the proverbial Thebes anymore. It's just too much trouble.

The "Author Income Sphinx" stands between us and a deeper understanding of our books, our marketing, and our money. Without a full command of these three things, any decision we make is just a guess. But if we can slip past the Sphinx, an entire world of insights is available to us, a world of untold riches and opportunities to sell more books.

But our Sphinx stands tall as she blocks our view of this splendid city, gnashing her teeth and flapping her wings furiously.

Let's hear her riddle:

"How can authors track their income in a way that is convenient and sustainable?"

Whatever you're thinking, don't say it. Our Sphinx is kinder than her Greek counterpart; she'll give as much time as we need to formulate an answer.

Let's creep away while she lies in the sand and sharpens her claws, and let's go on a journey to see if we can find the right answer.

Our author careers depend on it.

DIFFERENT PEOPLE, DIFFERENT PROBLEMS: THE STAKEHOLDERS

First, let's look at all the people who have a vested interest in this problem. It's not just authors.

Traditionally-Published Writers

Traditionally-published writers receive royalty statements from their publisher on a monthly, quarterly, or annual basis. A traditional publisher could be a large publisher or a small press. The statements may be printed and mailed, emailed as a PDF or Microsoft Excel file, or available on a sales dashboard for the author to review. Royalty statements have changed significantly over the years, so the longer an author has been publishing, the more likely they are to have seen many different versions of the publisher's royalty statements. This is because companies change their accounting programs due to obsolescence, inefficiency, contractual issues, or cost-savings.

(By the way, I am very careful in this book to distinguish between royalty reports and sales reports. Royalty reports are from publishers. Sales reports are from retailers. They are not the same and should *not* be used interchangeably. Check the Appendix for some context.)

Also, publishers can merge or be acquired, which creates another problem for traditionally-published writers because a change in ownership brings a change in payment and new royalty statements that may be more difficult to understand. The longer an author has been publishing, the more statements they have to keep track of. The publisher may have a payment threshold so that the author won't receive a check until royalties exceed the threshold. With some underperforming books, an author could go a long time between receiving royalty statements.

There are also literary agents, who work in tandem with the author and publisher. Sometimes publishers pay the author directly, but more often than not, the publisher pays the literary agent, who takes their commission and then passes the rest to the author.

Does the agent forward the publisher's royalty statement to the author or do they use their own? Does the agent have good accounting software to help them split royalties, or do they have to do it manually? How does the author verify that what they're looking at is the true amount owed to them? These are the issues traditionally-published writers have to wrestle with.

Literary Agents

Literary agents are also stakeholders in this problem. In my research for this book, I spoke with one of the largest literary agents in the country. This individual represents authors who are household names in several genres. We met because I spoke publicly about wrestling with this problem and they heard about it. The conversation was eye-opening.

Traditionally, literary agents take a commission from each sale. It is customary for traditional publishers to pay the agent. The agent deducts their commission and pays the remainder to the author. Common sense says it would be easier for the publisher to simply pay the agent *and* the author, but that's not how it's done unless the author negotiates it that way.

The agent I spoke to can't find good software to help with this problem. They explained that their publishers pay them every quarter. An assistant in the office has to manually calculate several hundred thousand dollars' worth of royalties and issue checks to authors. They're a reputable agency and they make sure the math is always right, but dividing royalties is a tedious task that they want an automated solution for.

In the hands of a bad or incompetent literary agent, you can see how this arrangement invites trouble (read: embezzlement).

Manually dividing royalties is further complicated by the fact that authors have different royalty arrangements—some authors command a higher royalty than others because of their stature or shrewd contract negotiation skills. Also, some authors are more prolific than others. It's hard work for the agent to reconcile all of money properly. Some agents are savvier than others, but the problem exists for all of them. The stakes are high—if they get the accounting wrong, they face lawsuits.

Traditional Publishers

Traditional publishers have hundreds, if not thousands of authors. They have to address this problem at scale. They dictate how royalty statements are generated, what the statements contain, how frequently they are distributed, as well as payment.

Royalties may be calculated by in-house staff or through the help of a third-party vendor.

Small presses may not have the technology to automate their royalties and therefore may have to calculate everything manually. The methods they use to create sales reports may not be industry-standard, resulting in reports that can't be easily run through software.

While publishers don't have a vested interest in solving this problem, they contribute to it.

Self-Published Writers

Self-published writers are not monolithic. We can divide them into groups, and some authors belong to multiple and even float between them.

Some self-published writers are exclusive to Amazon's Kindle Select Program (KDP Select). These authors publish all of their books on Amazon and therefore only receive sales reports from Amazon. These writers have it the easiest because Amazon provides thorough sales reports, and there are third party solutions such as Book Report that analyze and visualize sales data quickly.

Some self-published writers are not exclusive to Amazon, meaning that they publish their books "wide," at as many retailers as possible to maximize their reach and income. "Wide" authors receive many sales reports from many retailers.

Many self-published writers are not 100 percent exclusive or wide, however. It's not uncommon for writers to use KDP Select at some point in their career, whether it be at the beginning of their careers to grow a platform or on a book-by-book basis. Therefore, many authors intersect with KDP Select at various times throughout their career.

We also have self-published writers who are hybrid writers —meaning they have a mix of both traditionally-published *and* self-published books. They have the worst of both worlds, and double the work to collect all their royalty and sales reports.

We must also discuss another important cross-section of self-published writers, which are those who aren't making much money. These writers have an interest in solving the author income problem, but they're not making enough money to do anything about it. Or, the money is so low that they don't see a point.

There are also authors who have not published many books. These authors tend to manage their sales themselves, usually on a single spreadsheet. They're willing to do the hard work because they only have a few books and they don't view it as too labor-intensive. However, as these writers keep publishing, their systems will break down and they will either look for a solution or do nothing.

We also have prolific, busy, or successful self-published (and hybrid) writers who also have this problem. Money is usually not an obstacle for these writers. In fact, they may pay an assistant to calculate their sales for them. Or, they may also do nothing about the problem because the right solution hasn't presented itself yet. This group of authors has the biggest interest in the author income problem—not knowing how to manage their money is costing them money, and they know it. However, they don't know *how* to solve it, and they're not keen on learning the ins and outs of Excel. They are where they are because they're good writers. Their time is best spent writing and marketing.

And finally, we have a very small group of writers who are both successful and prolific, *and* technicians with data. Not only do they make a lot of money—they've also figured out how to solve the author income problem for themselves, either by paying someone to create a solution for them or because they're data literate. These writers still have little interest in solving the problem for the community, but they're still stakeholders because of the knowledge they hold. Only a handful of these authors are willing to share their knowledge with the community, mainly for fear of boring people.

Programmers

Authors aren't programmers. They don't have time to program.

Programmers (usually) aren't writers. They don't have time to write.

Programmers are always looking for ways to solve problems, however, and the author income problem is an interesting one, and a bonanza for whoever gets it right. Programmers are in a unique position to help, but there is another problem.

If you look at the writing community right now, most of the time, money, and attention goes to writing and marketing apps.

Everyone wants to feel productive. They want tools to help them write better and smarter because it makes them feel good about themselves. And of course everyone wants to make more money! These desires tap in to the human desires to be beautiful, rich, and powerful.

Because many writers are cost-conscious, they want to know that an app will give them a return on their investment by helping them sell more books. Writing and marketing apps fill that need. It's much harder outside of those two categories, even though there are big problems that need to be solved.

For this reason, apps that do not fall into writing and marketing are much harder to sell. This is also why there are only a few apps that help writers with their sales.

Also, programmers may not have the subject matter expertise to create these apps confidently.

Yet, as discussed above, many authors in the community suffer from the author income problem.

The current climate is a perfect storm, where authors suffer from a major problem, but aren't willing to spend money on it, and programmers don't feel that they can make sustainable income from an app that solves the problem.

Book Retailers

Book retailers are Amazon, Barnes & Noble, Apple, Google, and more. They allow writers to sell books in their stores and provide a monthly sales report to the writers. Like traditional publishers, they don't have a stake in the problem other than to ensure they are providing accurate and timely data. However, each retailer is different in the data it provides. Each retailer's sales report has different fields and captures those fields differently. "Units sold" on one report might be "Net Units Sold." Most retailers calculate exchange rates for the author; Amazon does not. Retailers may list book titles differently, such as some including the subtitle and others omitting it. While these items may seem trivial, they are vitally important. The diversity among reports increases the amount of data clean-up the author has to do to standardize the reports.

Book retailers include aggregators such as Draft2Digital and PublishDrive, who sell authors' books at many retailers that authors can't reach themselves in exchange for a small commission. The benefit to using a book aggregator is that you receive one sales report that details where you sold books for the month.

Many authors use book aggregators *in addition* to uploading their books directly to retailers like Amazon.

Bringing All the Stakeholders to the Table

Writers need a quick, easy, and effective way to calculate their sales reports to glean insights from them. Currently, they spend either an inordinate amount of time on the problem or no time at all because they don't have the skills or will to solve the problem. Their situation depends on the style in which they publish, where they publish, how many books they have published, and how much money they make. Both traditional and self-published writers have this problem; the degree varies on their circumstances.

Literary agents act as intermediaries between the traditional publisher and author, and they struggle to find an easy way to divide royalties.

Programmers want to find solutions to problems that they are passionate about, but the writing space is not lucrative at the moment because the market prefers writing and marketing solutions. They need to know that they'll make a good return on their investment.

Book retailers and traditional publishers supply the data needed to solve this problem, but that data is messy and inconsistent.

What would it take to align everyone's interests so that we could find a solution to the problem?

Let's look at the existing tools on the market to see what we can learn.

EXISTING SOLUTIONS: PROS AND CONS

In the business world, whenever an obvious product or service doesn't exist, it pays to ask why no one else has come up with the idea.

There's always someone smarter who's a few steps ahead of you. Why haven't *they* addressed the problem? Or have they? Why didn't it work?

My intent in this chapter is not to put down any of the current solutions on the market. Instead, I want to discuss their pros and cons so that we can see the problem more clearly.

Also, book sales apps are notoriously difficult to find. I encountered the following apps while on my journey to solve the author income problem—I know that there are others that I am not aware of.

There are only three ways to obtain sales data:

- **By downloading sales reports** from retailer dashboards and then doing something with them, such as manual data entry or Excel automation. This is the safest way but the most time-intensive.
- **By accessing retailer dashboards using**

author login credentials. There are services that will do this for you. This may be a violation of retailers' terms of service. Also, it requires you to give your passwords to third parties.

- **By using an Application Programming Interface (API).** Think of an API like a plug and a socket, where the retailer's server is the socket and the developer's program is the plug. The program connects to the retailer's server and downloads sales data according to the retailer's rules. Then the developer is free to do whatever they want with it. This is, without a doubt, the safest and easiest way to obtain sales report information. However, at the time of this writing, retailers don't offer this functionality to the author community, though the information could be made readily available.

Spreadsheet Templates

The easiest way to solve this problem in the short-term is with a spreadsheet template. I've seen many authors share the Microsoft Excel templates they use with the community.

The pros of spreadsheet templates are that you can borrow someone else's format. They may have thought of fields or organized their spreadsheet in a logical way that you never considered. These spreadsheets are usually free.

The cons of spreadsheet templates are that they rarely last long-term. As authors' sales (and books) grow, the spreadsheets can't keep up with them. Also, the spreadsheets can't overcome a major limitation—the bigger the spreadsheet, the more diffi-cult it becomes to manage it. Spreadsheet templates also require manual entry. You cannot transfer data from a sales report to your spreadsheet without doing it by hand. If you have one book, it's easy, but if you have fifty, it's tedious and cumbersome. Also, spreadsheet templates may or may not be organized in such a way that you can visualize the data within using charts. Authors who create them may or may not have advanced Excel expertise.

And then there's the old adage, which sums up the problem with this method succinctly: every spreadsheet is one step short of useful.

Advanced Spreadsheet Tools

Instead of a template, some authors have created spreadsheets with advanced macros that can combine sales reports into a single file.

A macro is a series of recorded steps that can be taught to computer software to allow it to execute the steps without a human doing so. An example would be using a macro to eliminate keystrokes. Let's say that you are an executive at a company and you receive a quarterly report with a bunch of extraneous information. You have to spend several minutes applying filters, deleting data, and sorting to get the information you need. You can create a macro that does all of this automatically for you in seconds so that all you have to do is click a button to activate it.

Macros are designed to automate work and save time. They're perfect for when you have reports that are exactly the same and you need something done to them. Fortunately, author sales reports are perfect use cases for macros.

Anyway, back to advanced spreadsheet tools.

Endeixis is one such provider. You tell them which retailers you sell your books at, and they create a custom spreadsheet for you encoded with macros as well as a recommended folder structure where you must store your reports. Each month, you place your sales reports in the proper folders and then, using buttons on the spreadsheet, Excel tabulates all of your sales. You can then manipulate the data to your heart's desire as well as take advantage of charts and graphs they program into the spreadsheet. Each month, you can add new sales with just a few clicks.

(At the time of this writing, it does not appear that Endeixis is supporting the tool. Their website is active, but they do not appear to be actively building it for people. They did not return my emails and the website hasn't been updated in a while.)

The pros of this method are that it takes away the data entry. The behind-the-scenes Excel work is not that complicated and could be replicated by someone skilled at the program. Authors could easily pay someone a few hundred dollars to create their own home-brew tool. The tool also has long-term potential.

The cons of this method (as Endeixis presents it) are that if anything goes wrong with the spreadsheet, either you or an Excel guru has to fix it. Most authors don't have macro skills.

Also, retailer sales reports change from time to time. For example, Amazon has changed its sales report format over time; its first generation lasted circa 2010 to June 2016, and then it implemented a new sales report from July 2016 onward that incorporated Kindle ebooks, CreateSpace, KDP Print, and Kindle Unlimited under one report, in a much more data-friendly format. It also changed the order of the columns.

The first generation of Kobo sales reports included one report for sales and another for refunds. In 2017, ebook sales and refunds were combined into a single report, and another report for Kobo Plus sales was created. Additionally, more columns were added to the ebook sales report.

These are examples of the ways that reports change over time. Even the most minor changes require attention because they can break macros. Macros *must* run the same way every time. Major changes require programming from the ground up to support the new "generation" of sales reports.

As retailer sales reports change in the future, the spreadsheet must grow to accommodate them, which means that you'll have to spend time adding additional functionality or paying someone to do it for you. For successful authors, this is a predictable expense that you can budget for each year. For authors on a budget, it may be more than they want to pay. The tool will always require work.

Also, this method doesn't take into account other author revenue streams such as Patreon, affiliate income from many different retailers, course sales, direct sales, traditional publisher royalty reports, and other unique ways that authors make money. For a nonfiction writer utilizing these channels, they would have to pay significantly more to customize their spreadsheet, if the programmer can even program the reports from these channels. The end result could be manual data entry for some reports, which defeats the purpose of automation. An optimistic author might say that if they can automate 99 percent of their sales reports, they can handle manual entry for the remaining 1 percent (or they can pay someone to do it). It depends on your preference.

Web-Based Aggregators

There are service providers who avoid spreadsheet work altogether and provide web-based access to your sales data.

These websites ask for your login credentials at the retailers where you sell your books. The website then pulls your sales data into a series of reports where you can view your sales reports in real-time. Some services may offer email notifications when your book is selling well.

Some of these aggregators are safer than others. Book Report, for example, gathers Amazon sales in compliance with the KDP terms of service (per the developer's claims). Many in the community use and trust Book Report, including many successful, full-time authors.

The pros of this method are that you don't have to do Excel work. You can view your sales from the comfort of your browser, close to real-time. It also eliminates the need to visit multiple dashboards to see your sales.

The cons of this method are that it may violate the retailers' terms of service. Retailers usually have language in their terms that says that you cannot grant a third party access to the retailer dashboard or give your password. This method may directly violate this language, and the developers may include hold harmless wording in *their* terms of service that prevent the author from taking legal action against them because the author is assuming the risk. Furthermore, the accuracy of these services can sometimes be questionable. They may not always provide the most up-to-date sales information.

Local Applications (such as Trackerbox)

A local application is a program you install on your computer as opposed to using it in the cloud.

Trackerbox, an app developed by Mark Fassett, deserves special mention. Trackerbox aggregates your sales reports into an easy-to-understand dashboard that gives you the essentials of your sales data. At the time of this writing, it is Windows-only. Mark successfully funded a Kickstarter to create a Mac version, but for unknown reasons, he did not finish it.

Authors feed their reports into Trackerbox. The program is local on your computer and the developer does not have access to your sales data, which makes it a secure solution. Trackerbox supports most major book retailers.

The pros of Trackerbox are that it's convenient and easy to use and secure. It will suit most authors' basic needs. It is also affordable.

The cons of Trackerbox are that the user interface is a bit dated at the time of this writing. Additionally, Trackerbox does not support alternative streams of income such as Patreon, affiliate earnings, direct sales (in-person or online), or course sales. You can track some sales reports manually, but that may not be desirable for most authors.

Trackerbox is also Windows-only, so if you want to use it on your Mac, you'll have to install Windows using Parallels or Apple Bootcamp. Authors may not be able to afford this, or they may not have computers powerful enough to install Windows on their Macs.

There's also the problem of Apple's new ARM chips—Bootcamp will no longer be a viable option after 2021 because Macs won't have Intel chips, and therefore cannot run Windows unless you use a virtual machine app like Parallels, if it works.

Another issue with Trackerbox is that it adulterates your sales data—you don't get access to *all* the fields in your sales reports except for the most important ones, such as title, author, units sold, and sales commission, to name a few. If you ever want access to other fields, you cannot see them in Trackerbox. This severely limits what you can do with your data. Also, in my brief testing of the app, there were other minor quirks with the way the sales reports are aggregated that may not be acceptable to data-savvy writers, particularly the way exchange rates are handled with Amazon. I'll discuss data adulteration later in the book, but suffice to say that if you use Trackerbox, you'll have to accept this trade-off.

That said, Mark is a pioneer in this space and he should be recognized as such. The author community owes a debt of gratitude to him for creating a workable solution to this problem.

Application Programming Interface (API)

This is the holy grail solution, but it doesn't exist yet.

If retailers made their sales data available via an API, a developer could create an app that could download it into a database. Once there, anything is possible.

Ideally, the API would only be available to an individual author, and not to the public. Each author would have their own unique API token.

The pros of this method are that it would unlock endless possibilities to help authors explore their data. It would be convenient and require no coding from the author. Also, it would be cost-effective for developers—they use APIs all the time. They could create an app that is local to your computer but uses your API token to download your data. This would be secure so that the developer never sees your data.

The cons of this method is that for it to work, *most if not all* retailers have to offer it. Otherwise, you have the patchwork problem mentioned with Trackerbox.

At the time of this writing, API access is a distant dream. I know of at least one team of developers who attempted to find sales data within retailers' APIs, but were unsuccessful because there were too many technical issues. Retailers don't make it easy today, and even if a developer could access sales data, it would likely be a violation of the API's terms of service.

But the tide will change. As we move into a future populated by the Internet of Things (IoT), technology will demand that devices be able to connect and interface with each other, driving APIs into our everyday lives. Web services are trending the same way, with companies like Zapier becoming ever-popular. Zapier connects web services to each other, like Mailchimp to Evernote, or Google Sheets to productivity apps like Asana.

In light of continued social media and marketing scandals, people will understand the inherent power of their data and want more access to it. As more successful authors grapple with the author income problem, they too will demand automated solutions for their sales. APIs can play a critical role in giving authors secure and convenient access to their data.

Customized Solutions

Sometimes authors don't use any of the above solutions. Sometimes they find their own solution to the problem. This might involve creating their own spreadsheet and keeping track of their sales manually, or paying an assistant to help them calculate their sales each month.

The pro of the custom method is that you can create a solution that specifically addresses your author situation.

The con of the custom method is that it can be expensive.

Bringing All the Methods Together

. . .

The existing solutions are as follows:

- Spreadsheet templates
- Advanced spreadsheet tools
- Web-based aggregators
- Local applications (such as Trackerbox)
- Application programming interfaces (APIs)

Now that we understand the approaches to gathering our sales data, it's time to talk about tools for analyzing it. And no discussion of sales data tools would be complete without discussing Microsoft Excel.

MICROSOFT EXCEL: THE ULTIMATE ANSWER?

Let's return to our riddle: "How can authors track their income in a way that is convenient and sustainable?"

When the Sphinx posed her riddle, I wouldn't have blamed you if you answered her simply with "Microsoft Excel."

You would have gotten your face ripped off, but I wouldn't have blamed you. But now we understand that the problem is far more complicated than firing up Microsoft Excel.

Microsoft Excel is a critical application. In my opinion, it is just as critical as the writing app you use. No writer making a significant amount of money can have a long-term career without at least an intermediate understanding of it.

Before I embarked on this journey, Excel scared me.

I used to joke that "Excel and writers don't mix." It's true, but no longer for me.

You're not going to hear me dissing Excel in this book.

But riddle me this: which version of Microsoft Excel do you use?

Are you using the most current version?

Are you on Windows or a Mac?

Are you using Excel or Power Query?

All three of these questions make a gigantic difference in what your *specific* answer to the riddle would be.

Older versions of Excel aren't as powerful and don't have the same features. If you're one of the rare people still using Windows XP or Windows Vista, you're missing out.

And let's take a moment to lament on how woefully inferior the Mac version of Excel is. It can't do *half* the things the Windows version can. The unfortunate part about this is that the features the Mac version lacks are features that writers need. The Mac version doesn't have Power Query, it lacks even the most rudimentary features like Find All, and it doesn't fully support macros. If you don't know what I just said, it's okay. I'll explain soon. I didn't know what these things were before I embarked on my adventure.

And no, Numbers on Mac is not sufficient to replace or compete with Excel.

The fact that the Mac version of Excel lacks Power Query is a nonstarter for anyone who truly wants to work with data.

Your sales are really just a data set. Whether you like it not, it's better to think of the author income problem as a data problem, not a money problem.

The Excel for Mac problem is exacerbated further by the fact that many people in the indie writing and creative communities use Macs. Macs are the go-to computers for creating content, and rightfully so. They're more reliable, suffer from fewer viruses, and prioritize convenience over technical prowess.

A lot of authors I know are buying Macs solely because they can write in the one true version of the Scrivener writing app and format beautiful ebooks and paperbacks with Vellum. You can write swiftly and format beautiful books on a Windows machine, of course, but many find that it's simply a better experience on a Mac.

I don't have any data to support the following statement, so consider it an educated guess. Let's say that half the writing community uses Macs.

That means that *half* of the writing community cannot use Excel in any meaningful fashion, not as far as data manipulation is concerned.

It is indeed possible to run Windows on your Mac, but that is a turn-off for some people because:

* They don't have enough hard drive space or memory on their computer to run Windows.

* Windows takes up too much space on their Mac, so even if they *could* run it, they choose not to.

* It costs money to run Windows on your Mac. You have to pay for an activation license, and, possibly, a virtual machine program like Parallels. You also have to invest in a keyboard that is compatible with Mac and Windows operating systems... trust me on this one.

* Some Mac users simply cannot stand Windows and wouldn't be caught dead with it on their computers.

* Some people have Windows computers at work and like working on a Mac because it feels like an escape. Windows reminds them of day job drudgery.

* Some Mac users don't even know that you *can* run Windows on your Mac despite it being a prominently advertised feature on Mac computers for the last decade.

* It looks too technical or difficult for the average user.

* Windows computers are more susceptible to viruses, so they don't want a backdoor on their Mac.

* Some users may consider *buying* a Windows computer instead, but many Windows computers are just as expensive as Macs these days, and most people don't have room for multiple computers. And, of course, viruses.

*   *   *

It's *a lot* to ask someone to run Windows on their Mac. If we accept my (educated) guess that 50 percent of self-published authors use Macs, we must exclude most of these authors from our journey because they would be unwilling or unable to do what is required.

From a business perspective, this is precisely why we don't have a killer local application that can help writers track their sales. It's too costly for an entrepreneurial developer to create both a Mac *and* a Windows solution. There be dragons on the web-based path too, as we discussed in the last chapter. And APIs aren't a viable solution yet.

If a developer *does* develop a solution for either Windows or Mac, they automatically alienate a large chunk of the author community. Additionally, Macs just don't do well with data, which is why the most viable solutions today are Windows-only.

To bring this back to Excel...the answer is that Excel *is* the answer to the riddle—or rather, part of it. However, we have to ask some additional questions to dig deeper into this under-rated and underappreciated tool.

GIVE ME A DATABASE OR GIVE ME DEATH

While we're on the topic of Microsoft Excel, let's also talk briefly about databases.

According to Merriam Webster, a database is a usually large collection of data organized especially for rapid search and retrieval (as by a computer).

According to Dictionary.com, a database is a comprehensive collection of related data organized for convenient access, generally in a computer; or, a data bank.

According to Wikipedia, a database is an organized collection of data, generally stored and accessed electronically from a computer system. Where databases are more complex, they are often developed using formal design and modeling techniques.

Wikipedia gives us additional information: a database management system (DBMS) is the software that interacts with end users, applications, and the database itself to capture and analyze the data.

Okay, let's unpack this.

Your sales reports are (usually) spreadsheets. Spreadsheets contain columns and rows of data.

You probably have a *lot* of spreadsheets to wade through. What do you do with them?

Each retailer has its own set of spreadsheets, usually spanning generations. A *generation* is a new iteration of a sales report, such as a design change or the addition or deletion of fields.

Each spreadsheet houses data. A spreadsheet is, in and of itself, a database, but your sales report is a poorly designed one. For starters, sales reports cannot be easily combined unless you take many steps to aggregate and standardize them.

Simple example: you want to know how many books you sold last year. You would have to go through each of your spreadsheets and tally up the numbers. Without Excel skills, you cannot combine your reports in their raw format. That's woefully inefficient.

A better way to house your data is in a database where the data from *all* of your sales reports lives.

A simple example of a database is your library's book catalog. The library contains a database with information of all the books it has. When you go to the library's website, you can search to see if a title is available. When you visit, the books you check out are marked as "checked out" in the database with a return date so that other patrons know when you will return them.

At a grocery store, the grocer must maintain a database of products, known as an inventory management system. Whenever a certain product is running low, the grocer must order more.

In both of these examples, databases help people make *decisions*. Library patrons use the library's database to determine which books are available; grocers use a database to determine which products are selling and when they need to be refreshed (among other things).

At its core, a database exists to house information for

retrieval later so you can make a decision. **That's how we need to be thinking about our sales—not as a bunch of spreadsheets but as a body of data; rather, a database.**

Spreadsheets also become cumbersome and clunkier the bigger they get, so while Microsoft Excel is part of the answer to this problem, there is another answer: relational databases.

According to the tech giant Oracle, on their website, "a **relational database** is a type of database that stores and provides access to data points that are related to one another. Relational databases are…an intuitive, straightforward way of representing data in tables."

Let's pretend we have a restaurant. The restaurant keeps records of who visits the restaurant and who orders what.

If we took the spreadsheet approach, we could save the following fields into a single spreadsheet:

- Date and Time
- Customer Name
- Server Name
- Food Ordered
- Amount Paid
- Tip

It would be easy to capture data in this manner, but after a couple of days, the spreadsheet would become beastly and difficult to wade through. Some of the fields would also be difficult to filter, such as Food Ordered. If multiple people enter data, then how do they handle Coca-Cola? Some might enter "Coca-Cola"; others "Coke"; and others "C." Some might accidentally misspell it! This is a nightmare.

If we were to approach this problem with a relational database, we would capture all of this information in a standardized way, but we would store it in different tables in a more granular nature that might look something like this:

- A table that stores customer information.
- A table that stores server information.
- A table that stores the menu items.
- A table that stores order information.

Instead of the first spreadsheet structure, which is short and wide, the tables in a relational database are tall and narrow. Each table has a "primary key," which is a unique ID that makes a data point unique identifiable. To illustrate this:

- In the customer table, each customer is given a unique customer ID.
- In the server table, each server is given a unique server ID.
- In the food table, each menu item is given a unique food ID.
- In the order table, each order is given a unique order ID.

You're probably thinking: That sounds complicated! But it's not if you understand why.

First, you're capturing all of the data at the point of sale. The data then gets divvied up by software into the necessary tables—you don't have to do any of that.

Second, storing data in smaller tables saves space. As a result, databases are space-efficient, and a relational database can scale almost infinitely with almost no loss in speed and performance—far better than a spreadsheet with the same data.

Third, storing data in smaller tables with unique IDs allows you to link tables together. Even though you have a bunch of tables, you can string them together to answer virtually any question you have. You can do this through a "query," which is a technical name for a data set that answers a certain question. Relational databases use Structured Query Language (SQL) in order to provide queries. Don't get hung up on the technical aspects; a query is simply asking a question and receiving a data set that answers it. SQL is a programming language that allows you ask your database questions; fortunately, it's quite user-friendly.

Let's say that the restaurant owner wants to know which customers visited the restaurant last Saturday. The owner would pull a query that includes:

- The customer table, which contains the first name, last name, email, and phone number of each customer.
- The order information table, which contains the date, time, amount paid, and tip.

The query now contains everything the owner needs to know about who visited last Saturday.

Next, the owner has more questions. Maybe there's a server that is causing problems and customers are complaining about him. The server worked last Saturday, so the owner wants to know what the average tip was per customer.

The owner could then, in just a few seconds, amend the query to add the server information table. Now the owner can see which server waited on each customer and the average tip. The query might reveal that the server's tips are lower than his peers', and therefore time to fire him. Or, it might reveal that despite the customer complaints and the server's prima donna attitude, he's bringing in the most tips. Maybe he needs a stern talking-to.

The relational database helps the restaurant owner arrive

at answers faster and more efficiently. The owner can slice and dice the database any way they want. They can even export their query to a spreadsheet that's far more manageable and contains only the data they need!

Imagine that, in your author business, you want to know how many books you sold last year. If you had a database, you'd simply query it. Your database could also answer specific questions like:

- How many books did I sell in Australia last year across all retailers?
- What's my refund rate?
- How much money did I make on Kobo during January of 20XX?
- On Audible, do I sell more books a la carte to Audible subscribers using their credits or Audible subscribers *not* using their credits?
- When are my slowest book sales months?

All of these questions can be answered with a well-organized, efficient database! Imagine how having answers to questions like these would revolutionize your marketing!

What is this sorcery, you ask? For most, it is none other than Microsoft Access. Access is a relational database management program that is built for storing data and querying. There are other alternatives to Access, but it is the most popular database program, used by businesses in all industries.

The mere mention of Access usually sends most people away screaming. That's why I was deliberate not to mention it until now…but it can play an important role in helping us solve the author income problem once and for all.

But for now, let's recap.

Microsoft Excel is part of the answer to the author income problem because it can help us manipulate our data.

Microsoft Access is another part of the answer because it can help us *manage* our data.

Continuing with our food analogy, Excel is like a knife. We can use it to chop our data up into manageable chunks we can consume. Microsoft Access is like a pantry where we store the data to retrieve it for later use. When we're ready, we can pick and choose the data "ingredients" we want to cook with.

Now that we understand databases, let's talk about our sales reports and how we can take them from a bunch of spreadsheets to data we can cook with.

THE DATA JOURNEY

Let's first understand the big picture of what we're trying to accomplish with our author income: **we need complete and accurate sales data in an easy-to-understand format so that we can ask questions of it and use the answers to make data-driven decisions.**

I challenge you to envision what your writing business would be like if you removed all barriers and could make data-driven decisions about your sales in seconds. What would you want to know? What would you want it to tell you?

The main problem with author income is that we think of it as a data entry problem. We do inefficient things in Excel, like take data from each of our sales reports and enter them *manually* into another spreadsheet that is poorly designed. Then we wonder why it's so laborious and time-consuming.

Data entry is only the beginning of the problem, not the true face of the problem—but it's so daunting and tedious that people give up. However, if they persisted, they would discover that data entry is the *hardest* part of the problem. Once you solve it, everything else falls into place quickly.

Once you move away from data entry, you move into the realm of data stewardship.

When you enter data, you can't see the big picture because you're focused on little things. Most people never get past this. Data entry is so tiring that when you're done, you don't have the mindset to analyze your data. Not meaningfully.

As a data steward, your job is to ensure the safe passage of *all* your data from point A (your sales dashboards) to point B (your sales database). As a steward, you can stay focused on the big picture and can zoom in to certain pixels as needed. You go from being reactive to proactive, and when you're proactive, you can see truth, strategize, and make better decisions that, to an outsider, may seem the opposite of what you should do, but is in fact the right path.

Stewardship of a database requires a different mindset that, when you adopt it, leads to opportunities because you can see more of them, more clearly.

Authors today are not data stewards. If they even address this problem, they are at best, data enterers—poor ones at best.

Let's consider the journey your data makes from retailer dashboard to database.

1. Collection
2. Import/Data Entry
3. Cleansing
4. Aggregation
5. Analysis
6. Action
7. Monitoring

You must first **collect** your data. This means downloading all of your sales reports from all the places where you make money. If you're a prolific author who has been publishing for a while like me, this is time-intensive. If you're a former traditionally-published writer, you may have *paper* copies of your royalty reports, or you may not even have all of your royalty reports. Everyone's situation is different but equally tedious.

You can start analyzing your statements right away, but raw sales data is difficult to interpret meaningfully (remember, stewardship). You have to **import** your statements somewhere else to get the bigger picture, such as Microsoft Excel or Microsoft Access.

This leads us to the cleansing step, where you must **clean** your data to make it usable.

When data comes to us, it's often messy, and we have to manipulate it in order to use it. For example, sales reports usually contain gross *and* net sales (accounting for refunds), but some don't. Some reports show refunds as a negative currency value; others show them as zero. We have to choose how we want the field to appear and clean reports accordingly.

Additionally, we have to make sure that all of the data is there and that none of it is missing or incorrect. In cleansing the data, we also standardize it.

Once you've imported your data into the correct place and cleaned it, you have to **aggregate** it, meaning that you need to join all your sales reports together. This is a surprisingly daunting task. To use a simple example, some sales reports call the amount of money you receive "sales" and others call it "royalties." Others may refer to it as "revenue." You have to ensure that all of the common fields have the same name so you can join all your reports together.

Once your data is imported, cleaned, and aggregated, the next step is to **analyze** it. Most authors never make it to this step, and those that do fizzle out because they've burned so many calories in the prior steps that they just want to be done.

But, my friends, this is actually where the magic BEGINS. The whole world is waiting for you now, assuming you have a complete and clean data set. Data analysis is about asking the right questions. With a complete and clean data set, you can ask nearly any question. It's actually easier to define what you CAN'T ASK than it is to define what you can. Ask the right questions and you'll get answers in the form of opportunities, which lead to more questions. Then you can **take action** on those opportunities and **monitor the results**, which leads to deeper **analysis.**

Another benefit of stewardship is that it is less about data and more about analysis. Authors can excel at analysis if given the chance. They just have to get there!

THE LOFTY GOAL OF ZERO DATA ENTRY

In order to use Microsoft Excel to its full capability without burning out, I suggest a radical idea.

In solving the author income problem, we need to aim for zero data entry.

This means (almost) no typing.

Imagine that you could download all your sales reports, feed them into a tool, and the tool takes care of the data entry for you, skipping you over the step of data entry, cleansing, and aggregation?

What if there was a tool that could:

- Import sales reports cleanly with no data missing.
- Clean and standardize the fields from *all* retailers' reports so they could be combined (i.e. all Amazon, Apple, Kobo, and others' reports could be combined into one place).
- Combine all retailers from a single retailer together (i.e. combine all Amazon sales reports together).
- Preserve all of your data, with none of it missing, even after cleaning and standardizing, so that you

could access it later if you wanted (i.e. no adulteration)

Sounds intimidating, doesn't it? I have good news: it's not. I created a prototype that obeyed all the steps above with only a basic understanding of Microsoft Excel and macros. Therefore, if an "Excel Elmer Fudd" like me can do it, then a developer can. I'll explain later, but for now, we need to understand the concepts.

Also, there is one key exception to this ask that we will discuss later.

We should demand no less than zero data entry from any tool that attempts to solve this problem. Data entry will turn off writers. Data analysis will energize them. If the tool cannot ensure zero data entry, we must reject it, or at the very least accept that it won't truly solve our problems. Data enterers can't be stewards.

To the developers and entrepreneurs who wish to liberate authors from the chains of the author income problem, to them I say: let us have an app that requires no data entry or let us have no app at all!

DATA CLEANSING CONUNDRUMS

We need to talk about data cleansing.

The topic of data cleansing can be quite technical, and I'm not going to shy away from the nitty gritty details, but I promise to explain everything in the simplest terms possible.

Data is a messy affair, and there are philosophical issues we need to address. If we get them right, we'll have clean and efficient databases; if we get them wrong, we'll create messy databases that won't do us any good.

DATA CLEANSING TOOLS: POWER QUERY OR MACROS

There are three ways to clean data.

First, data can be cleaned by programming—it happens behind the scenes without the writer having to do it. This is desirable, but outside the scope of this book.

Second, data can be cleaned using Excel's Power Query feature. Power Query is an underrated Windows-only feature that is in many ways a separate app in its own right. It allows you to take sloppy spreadsheets and clean them up so that they're usable and connectable. It's hard to do Power Query justice in writing, so I'll keep it simple.

Let's say that I have a spreadsheet columns titled Author, Book Title, Subtitle, Units Sold, and Sales.

It's unusual for a sales report to have a dedicated column for a book's subtitle. Some reports only include the title; others include both the title and subtitle in the same field; but rarely do you see a subtitle in its own field. That's going to cause problems down the road, so we want to concatenate (join together) the title and subtitle fields so that they appear together in one field.We can do this in Excel, but it's easier in Power Query. We can join the fields together for one report so that *all future reports we load into Power Query will automatically be formatted the same way with no extra work for us.* Just point Power Query at the folder containing all your spreadsheets and it will convert them instantly per your original instructions.

Another example is that Power Query can completely change the look of a spreadsheet. Let's take the Audible sales report. As far as formatting goes, the Audible report is the most daunting: it contains merged cells that are extremely difficult to break, a weird column structure, among other design decisions that make the reports difficult to read and use. In fact, the Audible sales report is a lesson in how *not* to provide sales reports. It's the worst one I've seen.

In order to make the Audible reports usable, we have to adjust the formatting so that all of the sales data is in clean columns and rows instead of oddly-placed triple columns. We can use Power Query to break all the formatting quirks of the original report and move the data around so that it looks like a more conventional spreadsheet. By the time Power Query is done with it, the sales report will be unrecognizable, but much easier to consume into a database.

Third, data can be cleaned using Microsoft Excel macros. Excel macros usually scare people—I'm hesitant to even mention them, but hear me out.

Excel macros can be created in two ways: first, using the Macro Recorder tool, which is not terribly useful; and second, in writing Visual Basic for Applications (VBA) code. VBA is the preferred way to handle macros.

Macros are automated recordings that tell Excel how to handle a document. Macros save you work by automating steps in Excel. For example, at the time of this writing, Amazon sales reports do not factor exchange rates into your sales numbers. This means that all of the currencies outside your home country will be grossly inaccurate, and you'll have no way of knowing how much you made per book.

You can write an Excel macro that automatically converts all of your book sales numbers to the values of your home currency using the exchange rates for the month you were paid. With some well-written lines of code and a click of a button, the macro will convert your reports in seconds, giving you instant knowledge of what you sold per book, with laser-like accuracy. You can even point the macro to a folder full of spreadsheets and it will convert all of them for you. Macros save an immense amount of time if used correctly, and author income sales reports are a *perfect macro use case.* Write a macro once, use it forever. Authors are just too scared to learn how to use them because they are very, very intimidating to novice Excel users.

However, what authors don't know is that you can hire Excel experts to create macros for you cheaply. On Fiverr.com, you can find someone who can create a done-for-you macro for around $20-50, sometimes less. You just have to tell them what you want.

When it comes to Power Query versus macros, a lot of people like Power Query because there's no coding involved. Power Query is easy to learn too. However, it's not quite as powerful as macros. There are some sales reports that can't be fixed using Power Query. Sometimes macros are the better answer.

It ultimately depends on what you want to do with your data after cleansing. If your goal is to use database software like Microsoft Access, macros are better. If you prefer to keep everything in Excel, Power Query will work best.

I'll discuss later in the book, but I found that a mix of Power Query *and* macros worked well for me. I found that macros worked on *most* sales reports; where they did not, Power Query did the job.

So, if you desire to walk this path yourself, you'll need to familiarize yourself with both Excel Power Query and macros.

There are YouTube videos, low-cost courses, and free blogs that can teach you how to use both competently.

Ask any data analyst about Power Query or macros, and they'll tell you everything you want to know. My experience is that most people do not know about them or even how to use them despite the fact that they can help a lot of people. Perhaps that's bad marketing on Microsoft's part, but for our purposes, it's helpful to understand these tools because we'll need them. Even if you choose not to go down this path, you'll still need an understanding of how they work.

MICROSOFT EXCEL VS. ACCESS: SIDE NOTE

In this book, I refer to Microsoft Excel and Microsoft Access often. It's worth noting that if you want to build a custom tool for yourself, you'll need to choose between Power Query and macros, but you don't *have* to use Access.

Excel is helpful if you want to keep everything in one ecosystem. The downside is if you accidentally delete your Excel spreadsheets, you'll delete your Power Query…

Microsoft Access is helpful if you want more future capabilities. This is my opinion only and it's not based on anything but emotion, but I find that my data *feels* safer in Access. Authors can use Access for other items in their writing business, such as print book order fulfillment for direct sales, creating a database to house the metadata for their books, or even for bulk upload of their books to a future book retailer. Access can do a lot of things that Excel can't. Even though it adds an extra step to the process, you're unlikely to go into Access unless you're looking at your sales, so you're less likely to screw anything up. Access also cooperates with Excel and accepts spreadsheets—even those that have Power Queries.

Should you pursue this path, the choice is yours.

DO YOU WANT ACCESS TO ALL YOUR DATA OR ONLY THE DATA YOU NEED?

The next question we need answer is whether you want access to all of your data or only the data you need.

It may seem like a strange question, but any and every sales report tool uses one method or the other. It's helpful think of them as unadulterated datasets versus adulterated datasets.

Unadulterated datasets are not changed. They contain all data included by the retailer. The important fields such as book title, author, units sold, and sales are included, but so are seemingly useless fields like VAT Tax Inclusive, VAT Tax Exclusive, Transaction Type, or Kobo's Cost of Goods Sold. In most cases, you'll never need these fields.

The pro of unadulterated datasets are that they are historical. If for some reason you ever lost your individual sales reports, as long as the dataset exists in your database, you won't need it because everything will be preserved. Additionally, you can "hide" fields you don't need.

The con of unadulterated datasets is that they require more work. Your database will have to store more fields. Some people may not see a reason to save a bunch of fields they'll never analyze. However, you may need that data in the future; if you don't preserve it, you'll lose it.

Adulterated datasets are changed from their original form. They contain only the most useful and necessary fields, such as book title, author, units sold, marketplace, and sales. Everything else is discarded. Trackerbox is an example of an adulterated dataset; you feed your sales reports into it, but it only shows you certain fields. You can't access anything else.

The pro of adulterated datasets are that they focus on what's most important. They take less time to program, which may result in cheaper development costs.

The con of adulterated datasets are that they're not complete. If you ever want the full dataset down the road, you can't get it. You're limited in the questions you can ask your data.

My preference, which should be the community's preference, is unadulterated datasets. No matter what tool we're using, we should always have access to all of our data. Whether we choose to use it is our prerogative.

Keep in mind that an author's career may last many decades; if the author ever loses their reports, it will be helpful to have the data stored securely in a database. Also, marketing is an evolving game; it's hard to anticipate the types of questions we will need to ask of our data in ten years. Therefore, it's better to retain it all in case we need it.

Authors should have unfettered access to their data, with the ability to hide fields they don't need.

THE AMAZON EXCHANGE RATE PROBLEM

This chapter is a public service announcement. I explained previously the biggest drawback to Amazon's sales reports: the lack of exchange rate calculation. This makes the reports unusable in their raw form.

I discovered a way to write a macro that takes care of this problem, and that's one way to handle it.

However, we need to make a demand to any developer who creates a sales report tool: it *must* calculate Amazon exchange rates. If not, then the tool is useless.

Amazon comprises the majority of most self-published writers' income. A tool that cannot get exchange rates right does not deserve to be adopted.

I wish it were that easy. Even if a developer were to tackle the exchange rate problem, they'd have a few dilemmas.

First, exchange rates vary by bank. Two banks directly across the street from each other can and do often have different exchange rates at the same point in time. Amazon's exchange rates are set by its bank, and they don't publish their exchange rates publicly, which makes this even more complicated.

Amazon doesn't make its exchange rates available through an API either, so the only way a developer can gather exchange rates is to rely on data that authors provide. Let's say that I shared my sales data with a developer so they could review my Amazon payment report to see the exchange rates for all the months in which I've been an author. I started publishing in 2014, so how will the developer obtain pre-2014 rates? And what happens in the months where I didn't get paid in a certain currency? Exchange rates won't be listed. A developer has to play a tricky game where they have to collect as much data from as many authors as they can, but their information will never be complete. Not to mention that authors have to share their personal data…

That way is unlikely to lead to any meaningful success. I'm not convinced that anyone could develop a *complete* database of historical Amazon exchange rates for every marketplace. It's too much work.

The developer *could* pick a reliable public domain historical exchange rate database and use the data from that, but my personal experience is that these databases are always higher or lower than Amazon's actual exchange rate in any given month. I have no idea what dictates Amazon's bank exchange rates because they never tracked consistently with publicly available historical data. If a developer gets this wrong, their conversions will be grossly inaccurate.

Or, the developer can look at a few authors' data and calculate the historical average for the exchange rates in each currency for the last decade of KDP's existence. This won't provide *perfect* conversion rates, but a ten-year average is enough to handle any major fluctuations in the currency.

This creates another dilemma for the developer: no matter how good an app is, it will never show the author the true, 100 percent correct Amazon sales numbers. There's nothing we can do about that, unfortunately, but the best we can hope for is an accurate conversion that gets us close. If it's high or low by a small margin, that's okay.

And let's also remember that because of rounding, we're also never going to see the true sales numbers either.

Amazon applies conversion rates at the marketplace level. So if you live in the United States and make 100 pounds *on Amazon*, Amazon will apply the conversion rate x 100 pounds. But that's not useful for us. We need currency conversions *at the book level*. In other words, if I sell 5 pounds of my science fiction novel book one, I need the currency applied against the 5 pounds so I know what the true sales commission is. For reasons I don't understand, Amazon doesn't work that way. I can calculate this manually, but it's a pain and tedious when you sell a lot of books in different Amazon marketplaces.

If we combine the exchange rate problem plus the usual rounding errors, we'll never have our true Amazon sales numbers, but that's okay. We just need to be close in either direction.

So, to recap, we must demand that developers of sales report tools apply a currency converter *at the book level*, and that converter should use a historical average for each of the Amazon marketplaces. This will ensure that the Amazon sales numbers will be as accurate as possible given the circumstances.

If the developer uses a public exchange rate database, we *must* scrutinize it and compare it to the actual Amazon exchange rates to verify accuracy.

We should also demand that Amazon apply a currency converter at the book level in its reports and also provide API access to its bank's historical exchange rates so that we can eliminate this problem altogether.

THE LITTLE STUFF: OTHER DATA PROBLEMS TO THINK ABOUT

We've covered the "big" data problems so far: Power Query versus macros, adulterated versus unadulterated datasets, and the Amazon exchange rate problem. But there are other, little problems with our sales data that we need to think about in order to ensure a clean database.

We must be data stewards, and the key skill of a steward is a keen eye. Since we're not doing data entry, we can look at our data from a big picture perspective as well as zoom in to any problematic pixels. Your sales reports are your domain, and you are responsible for it!

I can't cover every little issue that you have to think about because your situation will depend on your publishing arrangement, where you publish your books, and how you clean your data. But I'll talk about a few scenarios that will hopefully help you develop a steward's keen eye and show how you have to think about your data.

Date (and Time)

· · ·

The most fundamental sales questions involve dates. How many books did you sell last year? How many books did you sell last quarter? This requires you to track dates.

Databases prefer dates, but only a couple of sales reports tell you the date and/or time a book was sold. Most reports tell you what you sold in a given month.

Dates are a can of worms, so I'll try to keep the lid on this proverbial can. The short answer is that you'll have to pick a date format for your database. Do you default each sale to the first day of the month, such as 01/01/2020, or do you go with a month-year format such as 01-2020? There's no right or wrong answer. Just your preference. Database best practices dictate that you should have a separate column for month and year, but it's your choice.

Some reports include date and time together, which means you'll have to split them up in Power Query or with your macros.

(Oh, and by the way, using a date with the written month such as January 2020 is not a viable option. Databases work better with numerals. Plus, writing months out makes filtering a nightmare.)

Format

Do you want to run reports broken down by format? If so, you'll have to introduce this data into your reports as your reports don't tell you which sales are ebook, paperback, audiobook, and so on. Otherwise, you'll have to do a lot of clicking when you want to run ebook sales reports, for example.

.   .   .

Field Names

Some reports title the money you earn as "royalties." Others call it "revenue." Others still call it "publisher's share." This is a minor issue that we need to resolve.

Since we are housing all of our reports in a database, the fields need to have identical names or you won't be able to combine the different retailers' reports.

In Microsoft Access in particular, each retailer is a dataset that exists in its own table. You then combine each of the tables onto a separate "playground" table that contains the common fields that all the tables share. The "playground" table is where you run your queries, but more on that later.

Anyway, in order to combine tables, the retailer tables have to share common fields, and those fields have to have identical names. Otherwise, they can't be combined.

For this example, I chose "Income" and I made this the same on all the sales reports via macros. When my macros convert spreadsheets, they change "royalty," "revenue," and "publisher's share" to "income." This way, every report is consistent.

You'll have to do this for the common fields, such as Author, Royalty, Units Sold, Net Units Sold, and Country. Once you do this, you can combine all of your reports so that you can view Amazon, Kobo, Apple, and so on together in one place.

Field Values

As mentioned previously, we also have to address field formatting. How do you want to handle refunds? Kobo handles them differently than Amazon, for example. Also, some fields such as ISBNs get translated into Excel as scientific formulas. You'll need to be on the lookout for any fields that don't look right.

Book Title

Book titles seem relatively inoffensive, right? Consider this:

- Report A lists the title of your book only.
- Report B lists the title and subtitle of your book, separated by a colon.
- Report C lists the title, subtitle, and series name and number of your book.
- Report D (Audible) lists your book title, subtitle, series name and number, followed by (Unabridged).
- Report E includes your book title and subtitle but truncates the subtitle, making it incomplete.

Very messy. You can fix this problem with Power Query or macros if you know what you want the format to be and are okay sacrificing some of your data.

Country or Marketplace

Some retailer reports call the country where books are sold a "marketplace." Others call it "country" or "territory." We should have solved this problem above by changing the field name, but there's another, more sinister problem.

Some reports spell out the country name, such as United States or Germany. Other reports use a two letter code, like US or DE. Amazon reports use the Amazon link, such as Amazon.com or Amazon.de.

When you combine reports, and you want to know how many books you sold in Germany, you're going to have some line items that say Germany, others that say DE, and others that say Amazon.de. This, my friends, is the very picture of messy data.

We can solve this problem with quick "find and replace" code in a macro. We can also fix this with Power Query. Preferably, you'll change all your line items to say DE.

But there's another problem. Where do you stop? What about countries like the United Arab Emirates, or Turkey, or Botswana, or Romania? You're not likely to sell many books in these countries, but Apple and Google Play reports in particular have many, many different country codes.

The short answer is to convert the most common countries where you sell books and leave the others alone.

At the time of this writing, my primary countries would be the United States, the United Kingdom, Australia, Canada, New Zealand, Spain, Italy, Germany, France, South Africa, Mexico, Brazil, India, Japan, the Netherlands, and a couple others depending on your situation.

We have to make sure our countries are consistent in the reports or our reports won't be accurate!

Miscellaneous Payment Platforms

. . .

We also need to consider miscellaneous payment platforms. Affiliate links are the most common. Companies that pay affiliate commissions are just as diverse as book retailers, if not more. Affiliate commissions may not be a big part of a fiction writer's platform, but they're essential to most nonfiction authors and anyone who has a platform such as a blog, podcast, large social media following, or YouTube channel.

Amazon Associates is the universal affiliate service for authors and digital entrepreneurs. At the time of this writing, Amazon Associates offers a sales report that shows which items you referred to customers and the associated commission. This is great, but most (other affiliate platforms) don't provide line items in this level of detail, which means you have to do a lot of massaging to get the Amazon Associates reports to play nice with other affiliate reports *and* sit unadulterated in the database at the same time.

Other affiliate platforms do not provide sales reports (and operate on the honor system), or their sales reports don't have line items, so they're not useful. Or, they may not provide a report in Excel or CSV formats, which are preferred for data work.

Affiliate reports are the one area where authors run the danger of having to manually enter sales numbers. If you sell a lot of affiliate products like I do, you may find that the platforms are so diverse and you may not sell at *all* them with regularity, and it may not make sense to develop custom solutions for them.

We also need to consider platforms like Patreon, tip jar platforms, Google AdSense, Kickstarter, PayPal, direct platforms like Gumroad, Shopify, and Payhip, and course platforms such as Teachable, Thinkify, and Kajabi. The digital entrepreneur makes money from many different sources, and no revenue channel embodies this more than affiliate and miscellaneous platforms.

The challenge with these platforms for a developer is providing universal support. Every author's arrangement is different. It's probably impossible, especially when you consider that platforms frequently change their sales report formats too. Affiliate platforms are also notorious for going out of business.

Therefore, this is the only area where zero data entry may not be possible. But in my opinion, if a tool could support ALL of the common book retailers plus a handful of miscellaneous platforms, with the ability to do (easy and quick) manual data entry, that would be acceptable. From an author's perspective, you'd at least eliminate 90% or more of the data entry, and you could pay someone to do this for you. It would be far more affordable and efficient than outsourcing *everything*. Have an assistant sign a non-disclosure agreement (NDA), send them your affiliate reports each month, grant access to your database (which is far safer than granting access to your retailer dashboards), and pay them to enter the data accordingly. Or, you could do it yourself until you can afford to pay someone.

Due Diligence

Errors happen. You'll have to validate your reports to make sure that all of the data was imported correctly and that no errors happened in cleansing. As a steward, this isn't terribly fun, and it can be just as tedious as data entry, but the benefit is once you do it the first time, you'll know what to look for in the future.

Bringing It All Together

. . .

The issues in this chapter are problems you probably would never spot doing data entry. Even if you did spot them, there wouldn't be much you could do with the knowledge.

As stewards, we're in the position to fix these problems in the cleansing process. With a bit of effort, we can fix each of the problems mentioned in this chapter so that we can create squeaky-clean databases that are easy to query from.

BEAM ME UP, SCOTTY: YOUR DATA'S MOTHERSHIP

When you have a database of your sales data, it's your mothership. It's where everything lives. It is now your responsibility to patrol the mothership and make sure everything is running smoothly. This means inspecting your data for discrepancies at the macro and micro level, which is far easier to do once the database is built.

Now your concern is getting your data from the ground and up into the mothership. If you've created a solid database using Microsoft Excel or Access, importing your data is a simple process that just takes a few clicks per sales report.

There's another concept that will be helpful for you to understand. It's worth noting that while *all* your data lives in the same place, the process for accumulating your *historical* sales reports versus your *ongoing* sales reports may be different, particularly if you use Access.

Your historical sales reports are all of your sales reports up until the date you build your database.

Your ongoing sales reports are all of the reports you receive *after* your database is complete.

With Microsoft Access, you can import all of your historical reports with a few clicks once you've set your database up properly. But once your historical data is done, you have to follow a slightly different process for ongoing reports because of an Access quirk. It's not difficult, but it's a small distinction. This issue does not exist with Power Query.

Naturally, a well-built programming solution would eliminate this problem, giving you the ability to simply import any of your sales reports at any time. Trackerbox is an example of an application that bypasses this problem.

It's merely helpful for me to explain these concepts so you can understand how a sales report tool might work behind the scenes.

Anyway, you can now fulfill your duty as a data steward.

ANALYZING YOUR SALES: VISUALIZING YOUR DATA

Once we've solved the problem of data cleansing, it's time to do analysis. You now have a database with clean sales data from *all* your retailers—what do you do with it?

The short answer is "anything you want."

If you use Microsoft Access as your database, simply export the entire database to Microsoft Excel, and you can create graphs, charts, and pivot tables. It's so gratifying to see *everything in one place!*

You can use Microsoft Access to run individual queries too —maybe you want to know what your paperback refund rate is on Amazon. You can find that by querying the Access database, and then you can export to Excel.

If you use Excel as your database, you can create a "playground" file where you can do whatever you want with the data without worrying about what happens to the source.

I cannot understate how fun and insightful this is. There's nothing better than firing up a clean sales database and slicing and dicing it.

We could stop there, but we can now take our data analysis further.

Enter Microsoft PowerBI, the most underappreciated and unknown tool in Microsoft's product suite. BI stands for business intelligence. It allows businesses to take databases and datasets and visualize them in ways that Excel can only dream of. Businesses use PowerBI to great effect, particularly in large organizations. However, it's not part of the office suite and few people outside of data analysis circles know it exists. PowerBI is also free, which makes it even more awesome.

We can link our database to PowerBI and use its easy-to-use dashboards to create amazing visual dashboards in minutes.

Let's say that you want to know what your year-to-date sales and units sold, as well as a breakdown by format, territory, and title. You can do this in Excel, but it's a lot easier in Power BI. It takes less time too, because PowerBI will automatically update along with your database. Install the mobile app on your phone for insights on-the-go.

There are also other data visualization services, but they're usually quite expensive. There are others that you can find free on the Internet, but I would be wary of sharing your data with places that don't have a track record of security.

In short, once you reach the analysis step for your data, you can do anything you want. Almost anything is possible—all you have to do is dream of it and find a way to make the data do it.

This is the ultimate goal, and few authors are living it today because they're stuck doing data entry. This is the nirvana that we need to be asking for as an author community because it's possible. It doesn't have to cost a lot of money either. You just have to be willing to spend time, effort, or reasonable money on the problem.

If this is too much for you to do yourself, that's okay too. You now know what the standard should be.

THE TEST OF TIME

I have to take a moment to explain another problem that all databases and author tools face: systems break.

Retailers change their reports, Excel macros break, Microsoft Access suffers from weird quirks from time-to-time.

No system for amassing your sales reports will ever be perfect, be it something you do yourself or a tool that someone creates for the community. But we should demand that any tool we use can last for at least a decade. Why a decade? Because that's long enough to use a new tool and hang on long enough before you need to upgrade.

This is why a developer-created solution may not be the best option long-term. What happens if the developer dies, decides to move on to something else, or just stops supporting the tool? What happens to your data?

This is why I believe that the best way for authors to solve this problem is to roll up their sleeves and learn how to do it themselves. It's the only way it'll get done—done to the author's satisfaction—and stand a chance at lasting for more than a few years. Even though your author circumstances will change a lot in ten years, you can build a tool that will last for a long time with the right guidance.

Also, Microsoft Excel and Microsoft Access aren't going away any time soon. Chances are high they'll be around in ten, twenty, and even thirty years.

But regardless of how you decide to handle this problem, keep in mind that systems break over time, and be thinking about ways to proactively minimize that problem.

ONE WRITER'S ANSWER TO THE RIDDLE

We have now come to the inevitable part of the book where we must answer the Sphinx's question.

Before we do that, let me show you how I solved the author income problem for myself.

First, I have no background in data analysis or Microsoft Excel. I didn't know what macros, databases, or data cleansing was before I started working on this project. I am not a data person. Show this book to a data analyst, let them read a few chapters, and they'll verify that fact.

But I was suffering from this problem so much that I didn't accept no for an answer. I had to solve it or I knew that my author business could never get to the next level.

I purchased a LinkedIn Learning subscription and took several Excel and Access courses there. I watched hours and hours of YouTube videos and read dozens of blog posts to learn the basics.

I taught myself how to create macros, writing almost 10,000 lines of VBA code. That was NOT easy, but once you learn the lingo, you can search for done-for-you code on the Internet and you can copy and paste it and tweak it to suit your needs. I wrote macros that took the popular retailer sales reports and converted them into a format that I could plug into a database. I created a tool where I could point a macro at a folder full of sales reports, and in less than a minute, it would convert my past eight years of sales reports.

Some report macros were too difficult for me, so I paid someone on Fiverr to do them for me. I told them what I wanted, and in less than a day, they completed the work.

Macros were not an option for a couple of sales reports due to weird formatting quirks, so for the reports that didn't work with macros, I used Power Query, and it worked very well.

I then created a database in Access to load my reports into. Each retailer has its own dedicated table in the database, and I link all the retailer tables by the common fields: author name, title, net units sold, marketplace, format, and income. I upload my Power Query spreadsheets into Access and it accepts them and combines them accordingly.

I create a "query" that contains only the common fields. This gives me a report that contains everything I need to know.

I then export that query to Excel, and from Excel, I upload to Power BI.

It's a lot of steps, but I have:

- a clean database with all my sales from all retailers,
- a clean Excel sheet that I can do anything with, and
- a visual dashboard in Power BI that gives me a snapshot of my sales for the year.
- A data link between Excel and PowerBI that refreshes regularly.

Here's what it cost me.

About two months' worth of learning the programs

(working about four hours per day). If my time is worth $50, then it cost me $12,000 in labor. But we all know that this number is completely arbitrary.

About 240 hours. A standard novel takes me 40 hours, so I sacrificed 6 potential novels to create this solution. That's a lot of books I could have written during this time. I still wrote 10 books in 2020 (the year I made the tool), so I could afford to sacrifice a few…Honestly, most of this time was spent building a currency converter for Amazon reports and figuring out how to tame KDP's hellish "old" report. The rest of the retailers' reports fell into line very quickly afterward. Most are not complicated. Amazon KDP's "old" report, ACX's Sales Report, ACX's Bounty Report, and Smashwords's old reports (before getting acquired by Draft2Digital in 2022) are by far the most difficult reports to write macros for.

About $250 in programming costs to pay VBA experts to help me.

I had to build the macros and database about three times before I got it right. Someone with better data skills could build something better in less time.

I do have ongoing costs too. I'm sure to uncover issues from when I built it; for example, the ACX report is a colossal headache. I had everything working and converting properly, but for some reason, the macro stopped working before I wrote this book. I had to pay someone to fix that.

As retailers change their reports, I may need help from a VBA expert, which will cost me. Fortunately, I can find them on Fiverr for very cheap, usually with a 24-48 hour turn-around. After the first year, I'll be able to forecast the database's expected maintenance costs. I anticipate a few hundred dollars per year. Since I built the database, I can articulate what needs to be done in the macro code so I can hire programmers for just about everything now. So I'm not likely to need VBA skills anymore except for small items that I can fix myself.

The overall process of "doing" my sales every month takes around 30 to 60 minutes, which is significantly less than the 4-5 hours I was spending previously (doing data entry at that). I have to download my sales reports from all the retailers and load them into Microsoft Access, which takes around ten minutes for everything. Then I check for discrepancies and validate that the data arrived in the database correctly. Then I refresh my Excel file and check PowerBI.

I share these numbers not to brag, but to show you what it really costs to solve this problem. There are real time, monetary, emotional, and resource costs. These costs are not for the faint of heart, and I'm a unique personality type. Most people would not choose to endure this kind of work—but my pain level was high enough that I was willing to. Your pain level may vary.

Anyway, back to our Sphinx.

Instead of giving her an "answer" to the riddle, let's turn the beast's riddle upon herself and make demands. We'll tell her what we want and see how she reacts.

THE IDEAL SALES REPORT TOOL:
WHAT IT NEEDS TO HAVE AND WHY

I've heard many authors in the community say that they want a Vellum-like solution to the author income problem. If an app could just make it easy like Book Funnel made delivering ebooks easy, then it would sell itself.

Based on what I've explained so far, I don't believe it's possible without an API solution. No matter how you choose to solve this problem without it, there are significant tradeoffs.

On one hand, in accepting a tool from a developer, you trade convenience for flexibility. Few tools are likely to grant you the flexibility you will require as a full-time, successful author with many sales channels. And yes, I'm calling you a full-time, successful author, even if you're not, because you need a system that will evolve with you. A tool with the flexibility you truly need is likely too expensive for a developer to create, at least in the first iteration.

On the other hand, in building a tool for yourself, you have to be willing to survive the learning curve, and that's not easy. Not everyone is willing or able to do that, but a tailored solution is probably the right answer for most.

So here we are, back at the beginning. The Sphinx is

sharpening her claws, grinning at us as she anticipates our doom.

She asks a final time: "How can authors track their income in a way that is convenient and sustainable?"

Let us make our demands.

The Ideal Sales Report Tool

Right now, there is no tool that allows authors to track their sales uniformly, so the first answer to your riddle, dear Sphinx, is that each author must develop a solution that is unique to them.

As a community, the tool we need must have the following attributes.

First Principles

- The tool must be easy for even the most data-illiterate author to use.
- The tool must be equally usable by the beginning author and the bestselling author, and it must be able to flex over the course an author's career.
- The tool must recognize and respect authors' true roles as data stewards, not data enterers.
- The tool must be able to last any author for at least ten years.

Features the Tool Must Have

- The tool must make it easy for authors to feed their data into it, either from sales reports or via an API.
- The tool must be local to the author's computer. Web-based aggregation through obtaining authors' passwords is *never* acceptable.

- The tool must be as close to zero data entry as humanly possible.
- The app should support sales reports from *all* of the big book retailers: Amazon, Kobo, Barnes & Noble, Apple, Google, and so on.
- The tool must also include a simple way for authors to capture miscellaneous income, such as Patreon, direct sales, affiliate income, and more. While miscellaneous streams of income are diverse and hard to support broadly, they should be easy for the author to log in an alternative manner.
- The tool must be supported on an ongoing basis to account for changes that retailers make to their reports.
- The tool must support new retailer reports as new retailers enter the publishing zeitgeist.
- The tool must support legacy retailers and reports that are no longer in existence too, such as CreateSpace and PubIt.
- Whenever possible, the tool should acknowledge and support traditionally-published authors. While supporting their publisher's reports may not be possible, they should still be able to enter data into the tool.
- The tool *must* convert currencies *accurately* for Amazon sales reports or the data won't be accurate.

Authors and Their Data

- The tool must offer secure access to authors' sales since our data is our lifeblood. Integrity must never be an issue.
- The tool must not adulterate any data, ever. Authors must have full access to all of their data at

all times, though the app should allow them to choose what they see.

- The tool must follow database normalization best practices.
- The tool must allow authors to export their data to all common formats: Excel, CSV, PDF, and so on.
- The tool must provide clean data and must not create data problems.

The Sphinx's Response

The Sphinx is stunned, fellow author. She probably didn't expect such a logical and thorough argument!

She is not dying, so our riddle must not have been completely correct, but she also hasn't killed us yet, so it appears we weren't completely wrong either.

Her answer: "I shall take some time to consider your answer. I will let you know when I have made my decision."

And there we have it. We're stuck at the entrance to the proverbial Thebes, and we're not going anywhere soon, just like this problem.

Perhaps that's as it should be. I don't know about you, but I feel a lot better about the problem now. As a community, we now know how to approach it, what questions to ask, and what kinds of tools we should say NO to. That's the best we can ask as we wait for Sphinx to determine whether she wants to die or let us in.

In the meantime, let's talk about what we as a community can do to push the Sphinx to make her decision.

NEXT STEPS

There are many things the publishing community can do to solve the author income problem. This is the most complex, intricate, and messy problem of all time that authors have not solved as a group. As the world becomes more digital and our revenue sources become more diverse and numerous, we owe it to ourselves as a community to solve this problem, or we'll continue to struggle with money and data for a long time. We might even be left behind.

Here's what every key player in the industry can do to help usher in a new future for authors and their sales reports.

Traditional Publishers

- Develop a standardized royalty report for the entire industry to use, from small presses to large publishing corporations. Give the reports common fields, field names, and spatial locations for the common fields. Every publisher has different items they include, and that's okay, too, but as long as the standard items are the same everywhere, everyone wins. The medical industry did this with medical bills—no matter who the medical provider, medicals always have the same format and patients always know where to look for important things such as service date, amount due, billing address, and so on. If publishers did this for sales reports, it would drive standardization and make it easier for all authors to gain insights on their sales data.

- Pay both the agent and author separately. Stop relying on literary agents to disburse payment. Not only does it invite embezzlement, literary agents struggle with dividing payment.
- Provide easy access to legacy royalty reports for traditionally-published authors.
- Commit to a robust data retention policy that allows authors to access their sales reports for *at least* ten years if not indefinitely.

Book Retailers

- Adopt standard data fields with common names and data locations like traditional publishers so that authors can read reports easier and faster and different retailer reports can play nicely together in a database.
- Develop API access so that authors can download their sales data without having to log in to a dashboard. API access will drive the development of new and innovative tools.

- Continue commitment to robust data retention policies so that authors can always obtain their reports no matter how old the reports are.
- Convert currencies so that authors don't have to use multiple reports to figure out how much money they made.

Developers

- Commit to the security of authors' data.
- Engage the author community around a shared vision, with an eye to the future around automation and APIs.
- Communicate clearly what current technology can and cannot do.
- Recognize the diversity of author income, and that anything less than a complete solution is not likely to succeed.
- Commit to a multi-platform solution so that authors can use the tool no matter their operating system.

Authors

- Show developers that this solution deserves a robust app by pledging to pay for such a tool.
- Be vocal about what you want in a sales report app.
- Become data literate so that you can challenge

developers to create tools that will serve the community's needs.
- Recognize the convenience/flexibility trade-off.

These demands are a lot to ask for, but this is a *big* problem that all of us have a vested interest in solving.

Together, we can create a future where authors are data-driven and leverage the power of technology to make informed decisions about their author businesses. When they win, everyone wins.

And together, we can win.

Anyhow, I kept you alive from the Sphinx. Pay me back by sharing this book with your friends. If enough people start talking about this problem, then we might just solve it.

I've taught you everything I know about the author income problem. Now go and crunch those sales reports!

YOUR GUIDE TO SLAYING THE BEASTS OF THE WRITING WORLD

Do the "beasts" of the writing life trouble you? Fear, self-doubt, overwhelm, the inferiority complex, and more?

If so, you're not alone.

These "beasts" of the writing world want to destroy writers everywhere, but they can only hurt us if we let them.

This guide will teach you to do battle with the beasts that are sure to show up in your writing career. It will teach you to slay them once and for all.

- Fight **fear** with every ounce of your being
- Beat **burnout** at its own game
- Overcome feelings of **inadequacy and self-doubt**
- And more!

If you struggle with the "emotional" part of being a writer, The Indie Author Bestiary will be your sword.

This unique book takes the emotional challenges of writing, converts them into monsters, and teaches you how to defeat them.

Are you ready to conquer the beasts of the writing world?

Grab your copy of The Indie Author Bestiary at www.authorlevelup.com/bestiary.

APPENDIX: IMPORTANT TERMS

In this section, I define key terms used throughout the book in case you're not familiar.

This section is powered by my book, *The Indie Writer's Encyclopedia: All the Writing Terms You Need to Know*. Grab it at www.authorlevelup.com/encyclopedia.

Application Programming Interface (API): a set cf rules that allows programmers to develop software for a particular operating system without having to be completely familiar with that operating system (from Merriam Webster).

APIs allow developers to connect with retailers' servers and download data.

Database: According to Merriam Webster, a database is a usually large collection of data organized especially for rapid search and retrieval (as by a computer).

According to Dictionary.com, a database is a comprehensive collection of related data organized for convenient access, generally in a computer; or, a data bank.

According to Wikipedia, a database is an organized collection of data, generally stored and accessed electronically from a computer system. Where databases are more complex, they are often developed using formal design and modeling techniques.

Wikipedia gives us additional information: a database management system (**DBMS**) is the software that interacts with end users, applications, and the database itself to capture and analyze the data.

Generation: Each iteration of a retailer's sales report. Any time the retailer makes even a minor change, it spawns a new generation of reports. Developers must respond accordingly with new programming to adapt to the change. With a self-made solution, you will have to update your macros or Power Query as well.

Macro: In Microsoft Excel, a series of steps programmed into the software that can be executed with a simple command. Macros can be created with the Macro Recorder or with Visual Basic for Applications (VBA) code.

Query: In a database, a set of data that meets certain parameters asked by the retriever.

Royalty: A sum paid to a copyright or patent holder by a licensee for use of the rights; for authors, this sum is a percentage of income from each copy of a book sold

Amazon and other online book retailers do not technically pay out "royalties," though they call them that. A royalty requires you to license your rights in exchange for a percentage of income for each book sold, and self-published authors do not license their rights to online book retailers when they publish on those platforms. Therefore, the accurate definition for online book retailer payments is "sales commissions."

For this reason, publishers issue royalty reports and retailers issue sales reports. The two terms should not be used interchangeably.

Structured Query Language (SQL): Pronounced "sequel." The programming language in which queries are written (see "query" definition.)

MEET M.L. RONN

Science fiction and fantasy on the wild side!

M.L. Ronn (Michael La Ronn) is the author of many science fiction and fantasy novels including *The Good Necromancer*, *Android X,* and *The Last Dragon Lord* series.

In 2012, a life-threatening illness made him realize that storytelling was his #1 passion. He's devoted his life to writing ever since, making up whatever story makes him fall out of his chair laughing the hardest. Every day.

Learn more about Michael
www.authorlevelup.com (for writers)
www.michaellaronn.com (fiction)

MORE BOOKS BY M.L. RONN

Books for Writers

Indie Author Confidential (Series)
    How to Write Your First Novel
    Be a Writing Machine
    Mental Models for Writers
    The Indie Writer's Encyclopedia
    The Indie Author Atlas
    The Indie Author Bestiary
    The Reader's Bill of Rights
    The Self-Publishing Compendium
    150 Self-Publishing Questions Answered
    Authors, Steal This Book
    The Indie Author Strategy Guide
    How to Dictate a Book
    Advanced Author Editing
    Keep Your Books Selling
    The Author Estate Handbook
    The Author Heir Handbook

Interactive Fiction: How to Engage Readers and Push the Boundaries of Story Telling
Indie Poet Rock Star
Indie Poet Formatting
2016 Indie Author State of the Union

More Books for Writers:

www.authorlevelup.com/books

Fiction:

www.michaellaronn.com/books